Projects Inspired by

Céline George

Acknowledgements

The author and publishers would like to thank the children of Cross-in-Hand Primary School, Mayfield Primary School and Stonegate Primary School for their artwork. They would also like to give a special thanks to the children in Cross-in-Hand Art Club and to Philip George, Hazel Hegarty and Holly Morley for their artwork.

The author and publishers would also like to thank these teachers for their expertise and practical help: Sue Dean, Sian Faulkner, Louise Owen, Mary Westhead, Linda Sheffield, Peter Pettigrew, Sian Collison, Benjamin Hawkes and Jennifer Causer. They would like to thank Nikki Skinner and Sarah Matthews for running the Art Club, Vickie Brickle for her expert help and Emma Gordon for her inspiration.

The author and publishers would particularly like to thank these artists who contributed their ideas for the book: Michael Cruickshank, Daphne Todd and Kate Malone.

Finally, they would like to thank Stephanie Jephson and Sophie George for their creative inspiration and for their expert help.

Fabric Picture (page 9)

Published by Collins, An imprint of HarperCollins*Publishers*
77 – 85 Fulham Palace Road, Hammersmith, London, W6 8JB

Browse the complete Collins catalogue at
www.collinseducation.com

© HarperCollins*Publishers* Limited 2011
Previously published in 2004 by Folens as 'Inspired by Art'
First published in 2004 by Belair Publications

10 9 8 7 6 5 4 3 2 1

ISBN-13 978-0-00-743942-3

Céline George asserts her moral rights to be identified as the author of this work

All rights reserved. No part of this publication may be reproduced, stored in a retrieval system, or transmitted in any form or by any means, electronic, mechanical, photocopying, recording or otherwise, without the prior written permission of the Publisher or a licence permitting restricted copying in the United Kingdom issued by the Copyright Licensing Agency Ltd., 90 Tottenham Court Road, London W1T 4LP.

British Library Cataloguing in Publication Data
A Catalogue record for this publication is available from the British Library

Every effort has been made to trace copyright holders and to obtain their permission for the use of copyright material. The authors and publishers will gladly receive any information enabling them to rectify any error or omission in subsequent editions.

Commissioning Editor: Zoë Nichols   Editor: Caroline Marmo   Cover design: Mount Deluxe
Page Layout: Suzanne Ward   Photography: Kelvin Freeman

Printed and bound by Printing Express Limited, Hong Kong

Contents

Introduction   4

Textiles and Materials
Janet Bolton   6
Stephanie Jephson   10

Landscape
David Hockney   14
Michael Cruickshank   18

Sculpture
Pablo Picasso   22
Henry Moore   26

Imagination
Raymond Briggs   30

Containers and Objects
Kate Malone   34
Paul Cézanne   38
Pierre-Auguste Renoir   42

Portrait
Pablo Picasso   46
Daphne Todd   50

Nature
Henri Matisse   54
Allina Khumalo Ndebele   58

Portraying Relationships
Paula Rego   62
David Hockney   66
Gary Blythe   70

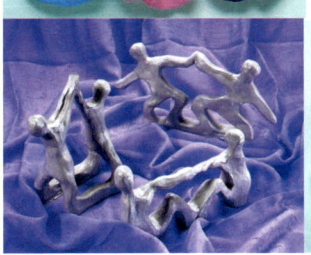

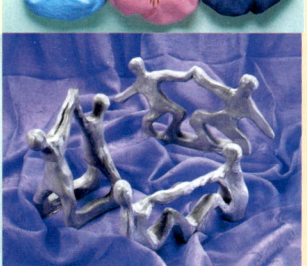

3

Introduction

Projects Inspired by Artists uses the painting, sculpture, textile design, book illustration and ceramics of famous artists as a starting point for children's artwork. The aim of the book is to use the artist's work as a source of inspiration, encouraging children's creativity through a range of activities in art and design. All the artists' work has been carefully chosen to reflect the different elements of the Art curriculum. The themes within a chapter cover a variety of skills, including drawing portraits, landscape painting, sewing wall hangings, and creating sculpture in a number of ways using clay, papier-mâché and modroc. Ideas for display are also given. Most chapters include an element of three-dimensional work, some of which have a practical value as well as a creative one. An example of this is the animal cushions inspired by Allina Ndebele's tapestry Mpisi and the Lion (page 61) and the pineapple clay containers inspired by Kate Malone's Choir Boy and Choir Girl Pineapple (page 37).

Using the Pictures

Each theme provides a complete project of four or five activities all linked to the artist's work shown at the start of the theme. Activities are designed to be suitable for whole class or small group work, depending on the preference of the teacher.

Teachers should use the artist's work as a starting point for whole class discussion. Suggestions are made to focus the children to particular elements of the artwork prior to commencing the activity. I recommend that the artist's work also be discussed generally in terms of composition, colour, texture and mood before starting the project.

As the approach used in this book looks at artwork as a process (i.e. working through different stages before the final piece is completed) it is recommended that each theme be taught as a complete project over several weeks. This is because all the activities within a theme are closely linked and new skills are practised and developed, culminating in a final piece of artwork or display. As this book is closely linked to the Art and Design curriculum, it could be used either for weekly art sessions or as a basis for innovative work in an after-school art club.

Inviting Artists into School

When children are given the opportunity to work alongside artists they are highly motivated and their work is greatly enhanced. Many artists are only too delighted to become involved in children's artwork, especially when their work is being used as a valued resource and starting point.

In this book artists were invited to give presentations about their work and to contribute to an art lesson. The landscape artist, Michael Cruickshank, inspired children to produce their own watercolour landscapes using the local church as a focal point. He explained the process of painting starting from his initial sketch of a scene through to framing and exhibiting it in his gallery. The textile artist, Stephanie Jephson, suggested different ways of displaying artwork and recommended entering children's textile work in competitions. The portrait artist, Daphne Todd, gave a presentation to the children about her work. It is easy to contact artists to enquire about visits to schools as their details can usually be found on the Internet.

Further Ideas to Enhance Artwork

Some of the artists in this book are living artists and their work is very accessible. It is also possible to carry out further research on all of the artists through a variety of ways:

- using the Internet
- visiting galleries
- using libraries
- attending exhibitions.

I hope that you will enjoy using this book and that you will in turn be inspired to help children create their own exciting and innovative artworks.

Céline George

Textiles and Materials

Janet Bolton (1942–)

Behind Our Back Garden, 1995, fabric collage sewn by hand, by Janet Bolton (1942–) © Janet Bolton

Janet Bolton is a decorative artist who creates small, fabric pictures using appliqué and a variety of stitching techniques. She grew up in Lancashire, England, where fabric making was once the main industry of the area. Janet studied Fine Art at college where she was introduced to working with textiles. She does not believe in forcing ideas but allows them to develop naturally, saying, 'Things that happen the most easily are often the best. It's often the first placing of a shape that turns out to be the most successful.'

In this fabric picture, Behind Our Back Garden, Janet Bolton has used one of her favourite themes, kite flying. The composition of the picture is the most important part of her work. The kite shapes overlap the borders but the finished result is uncluttered. Each shape and colour has been carefully positioned and every stitch applied with a great deal of thought to the overall effect. She has framed the picture using a selection of fabrics that have been sewn together. Her work has an almost childlike simplicity.

Textiles and Materials

Outdoor Sketches

Janet Bolton spends a lot of time observing and sketching before she begins her work. Her ideas develop from looking at everyday objects and views, for example bees, sheep, bowls of flowers and kite flying.

Resources
- A4 sketch paper or sketchbooks
- Sketch pencils

Approach

1. Look at Janet Bolton's fabric picture Behind Our Back Garden on page 6 and discuss the different parts that make up the complete work.
2. Discuss the areas in the local community where the children play outdoors. This might include gardens, parks or school playing fields. What games do they enjoy playing?
3. If possible, go outside and observe features in the school environment.
4. Sketch pictures of a garden or park, showing buildings, plants, trees and people playing an outdoor game.

Garden Paper Weaving

Resources
- Pictures of gardens
- Pre-cut coloured card
- 2cm strips of a variety of paper for weaving e.g. wrapping paper, crêpe paper, tissue paper, sugar paper, newspaper and foil

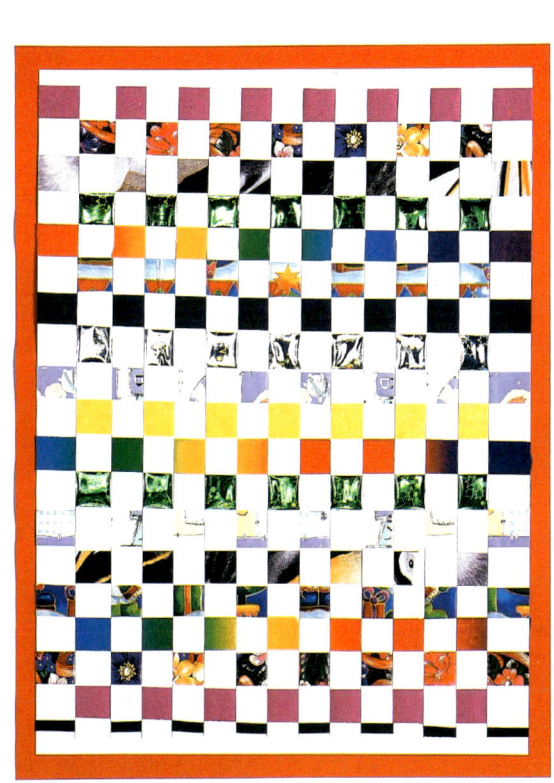

Approach

1. Discuss the colours seen in outside environments, particularly those found in gardens. If possible, look at different pictures of gardens for inspiration. Make a collection of different types of coloured paper.
2. Fold a piece of A4 card in half.
3. Cut strips approximately 2cm apart, making sure a 2cm border is left at the top and the sides.
4. Using a variety of paper, weave the strips in and out across the card to create a colourful garden weaving.

Textile Weaving

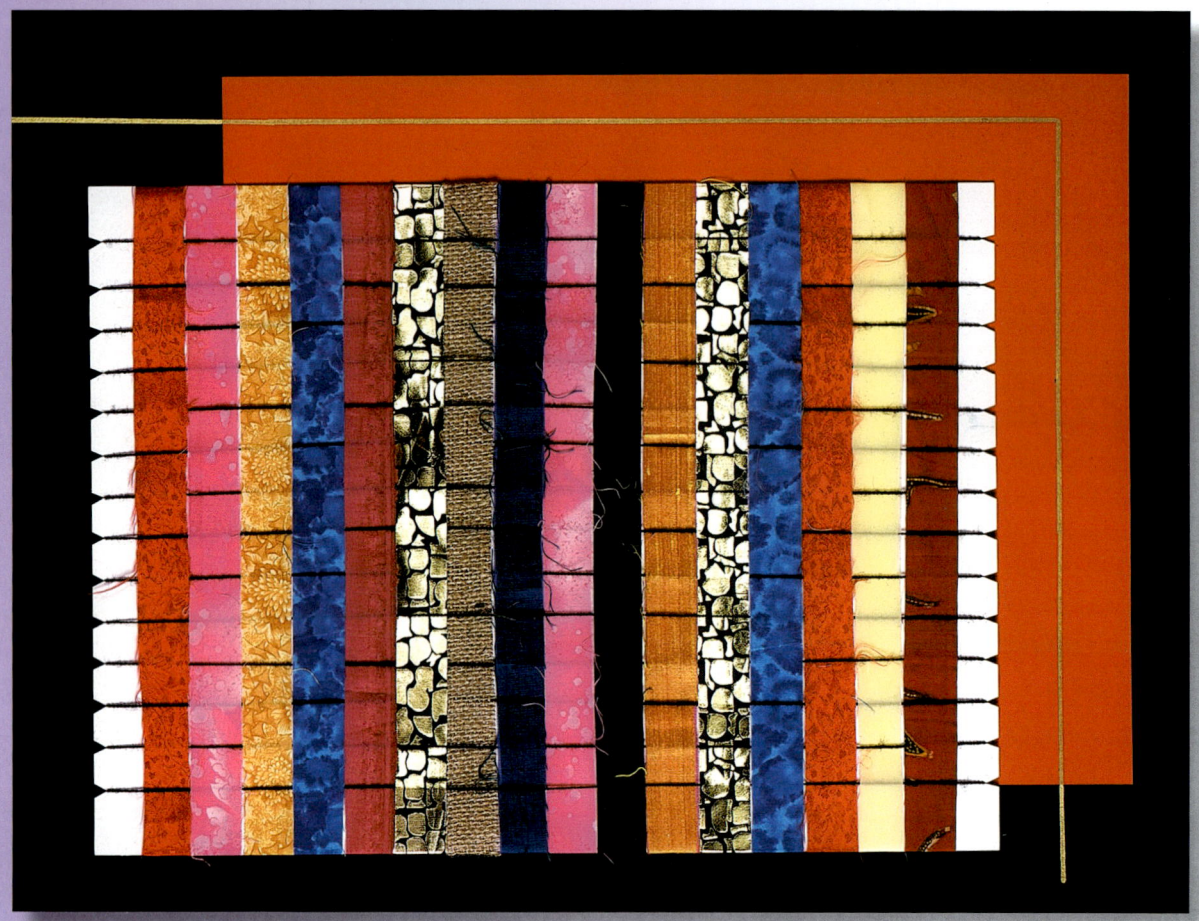

Resources
- Prepared card loom
- Strips of fabric in a variety of colours and textures (3cm wide), e.g. cotton, silk, calico, hessian, velvet, linen, net

Approach

1. Weave the strips of fabric across the loom.
2. Use a variety of sequences, for example in and out, over two and under one.
3. Arrange the strips of fabric to create different textures.

Janet Bolton uses the weave of the fabric to produce texture in her pictures. She sometimes creates the background by mixing and matching the weave of the fabric before joining the pieces together, as can be seen in Behind Our Back Garden.

Making a Loom

To make a simple card loom, cut the same number of notches at either end. On the back of the card, in the top left-hand corner, secure the wool. Working across the card, wind the wool using the notches as a guide to make the warp. When this process is complete, secure the end at the back of the loom. It is best if children work collaboratively in groups of about six.

Textiles and Materials

Fabric Picture

Janet Bolton uses a fabric background on to which textile shapes are sewn to create a picture. She then attaches a border, which can be one complete piece of fabric or a selection sewn together.

Resources
- 25cm² pieces of calico
- Patterned cotton fabric cut into squares, circles, triangles, rectangles and strips
- Wool
- Ribbon
- Fabric glue
- Scissors for cutting fabric
- Sketches from page 7

Approach

1. Look again at Behind Our Back Garden and the outdoor sketches from the activity on page 7. Talk about how the children could create their own fabric picture. Focus on the different components of the piece, such as the background, border and individual shapes.
2. Fold over the top third of the calico and cut weaving slots.
3. Use the original outdoor sketch and select the fabrics required for the picture.
4. Weave strips of fabrics across the calico on to the background to make the sky.
5. Cut out and arrange shapes of fabric on to the background to make the picture.

6. Glue the pieces of fabric to the background.
7. Select strips of fabric and glue around the outside of the picture to create a border.
8. Older children could use stitching instead of glue to attach the fabric pieces on to the background.

9

Stephanie Jephson (1951–)

Secret Garden 1 by Stephanie Jephson (1951–), 2002 © Stephanie Jephson

Stephanie Jephson was born in Zambia, and grew up in Zimbabwe, Africa. She moved to Saudi Arabia in 1985, where she lived for three years with her husband and two small sons until they moved to Sussex, England, in 1987. She is a textile designer who became interested in art and fabric design while studying to become an infant teacher. She has worked with many textile artists and has produced a variety of fabric designs such as wall hangings, patchwork quilts and wearable art.

This wall hanging was created using natural fabrics and has been divided into six main sections. She says, 'I gave the wall hanging its name because it reminded me of a "secret garden" my mother had created. The idea that something is waiting to be discovered appeals to me and in this piece of work every time you look at it you see something new.'

Each of the areas represents a part of the garden – favourite flowers, pathways and a stream. The design was built up by layering pieces of fabric, leaving the edges raw. A variety of cotton threads were used to secure the pieces and decorative stitching was added where required. Before the piece was dyed, Stephanie chose the colours she wanted to fit in with her image of the garden. Finally, beads, sequins, buttons and a variety of threads were used to embellish and finish the work.

Textiles and Materials

Paper Garden Collage

Resources
- Coloured card
- Pictures of flowers, shrubs, ponds, walls and fences from magazines or wallpaper
- Glue
- Scissors

Approach

1. In Secret Garden 1, Jephson uses colour, shape and texture to communicate her ideas and feelings. Look at her wall hanging and discuss the ways in which these ideas could be created using a different medium such as paper.
2. Cut or tear out a selection of the garden pictures.
3. Using a variety of these pictures, experiment with a composition to create an impression of a garden.
4. Arrange the pictures on a card background.
5. Glue the pieces of paper to the card.

Textured Fabric Image

Resources
- Coloured card
- Small pieces of fabric in an assortment of shapes and contrasting textures, e.g. cotton, calico, linen, hessian silk and velvet
- Glue
- Sequins
- Storybooks containing garden images

Approach

1. Examine how Jephson uses the different textiles to create a garden image in her Secret Garden 1. Do the children know any stories that contain a magical or secret garden? An example could be The Selfish Giant by Oscar Wilde (published by Puffin).
2. Choose an image of a garden from a story that shows the changing seasons, for example frost, pink and pearl blossoms, snow and autumn fruit.
3. Select pieces of fabric to create the image of a garden.
4. Match the colours, shapes and textures to the image.

5. Try various patterns before gluing them down on to the card.
6. Glue the fabric arrangement on to the card.

Fabric Dye Flowers

Resources
- Pre-washed calico or white cotton squares (20cm^2)
- Cold water dyes: turquoise, red and yellow
- Cold dye fix
- Plastic tray
- Rubber gloves
- Tissue paper
- Coloured card
- A selection of thread
- Large-eyed needles
- Pins, buttons, bugle beads and sequins

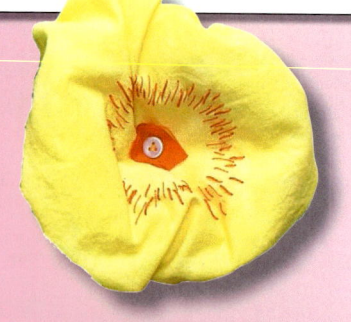

Approach

1. Look at the way Jephson uses dye to enhance her hanging in *Secret Garden 1*. Talk about fabric dyeing and examine some pre-dyed garments.
2. Work in a well-ventilated area. Put on the rubber gloves. Dye the pieces of fabric using the three suggested colours.
3. Once the fabric is ready, wash in hot, soapy water and rinse again until the water runs clear. Allow to dry.
4. Repeat the process if paler shades are needed.
5. Scrunch up a selection of the dyed fabric pieces to create flower shapes.
6. Place tissue paper behind the fabric pieces to create a 3D effect.
7. Pin the scrunched-up fabric to a piece of card.
8. Fix the final arrangement in place using large stitches and thick, colourful thread.
9. Embellish boldly with sequins, buttons and bugle beads.

Garden Wall Hanging

Approach

1. Create a textile wall hanging like Jephson's or, alternatively, one based on a storybook garden, such as *The Selfish Giant* from the activity on page 11.
2. The hanging has six panels. Each panel should represent a different garden image, perhaps showing a different season.
3. Using a small calico square as the base of the panel, select a variety of fabrics to represent the colours required in the garden at a specific time of year.

Textiles and Materials

Resources
- Large piece of calico
- Smaller pieces of dyed calico (20cm^2)
- Small pieces of fabric in an assortment of shapes and contrasting textures e.g. braiding, lace, silk, jute, scrim, muslin, hessian, cotton, calico and linen
- Beads, buttons and sequins
- Old necklaces
- Selection of threads e.g. cotton, embroidery, wool, ribbon and string
- Tapestry and large-eyed needles
- Scissors

4. Create texture by folding, scrunching, layering and pleating the fabrics. Arrange the fabric to make a final design and stitch the pieces of fabric on to the calico square, using a variety of threads.
5. Embellish the design by stitching on buttons, sequins and glass beads for decoration.
6. Stitch the children's panels together to produce a colourful garden wall hanging.

Landscape
David Hockney (1937–)

David Hockney *"California Bank"* 1964, acyrlic on canvas 30×25" © David Hockney

David Hockney was born in the industrial town of Bradford in the north of England. He won the gold medal for his year at the Royal College of Art and by the time he reached his mid-twenties he had become a famous artist. After finishing art school in London, he moved to California in the United States of America. David Hockney is Britain's most celebrated living artist.

In this painting, *California Bank*, David Hockney has used vertical strips of colour overlapping other shapes almost like a piece of weaving. The image is simple, in which the foreground of the building has darker tones than the background. The vertical strips become lighter towards the top of the building, creating depth.

Paper Weaving

Resources
- A3 Black sugar paper
- A3 Sugar paper in an assortment of blues, mauves and pinks
- Scissors
- Glue

Landscape

Approach

1. Look at David Hockney's painting, *California Bank*. The foreground of the building has darker tones than the background. Discuss creating this effect through weaving using different tones of paper.

2. Place a sheet of black sugar paper in a portrait position and fold in half.

3. Starting from the folded line, cut strips into the paper, making sure to leave a wide border on all sides.

4. Cut the sheets of coloured sugar paper lengthwise to form strips.

5. Open up the black sugar paper and weave the coloured paper strips between the slits.

6. Make sure that the foreground has darker colours than the background.

7. Graduate the colours so that the lightest is at the top.

Building Sketches

Resources
- A4 Sketch paper
- Sketch pencils
- Fine-line felt-tipped pen
- Photographs or paintings of buildings in an urban setting
- Viewfinder (see page 19)

1. Look at David Hockney's *California Bank* and focus on his use of blocks of strips and squares.

2. Choose a photograph or a painting of a building in an urban setting and sketch the outline.

3. Using a viewfinder, focus on a section of the building.

4. Using different shapes to represent windows, fill in the details of the building.

5. Outline the complete sketch, using a fine-line felt-tipped pen.

15

Paper and Fabric Collage Buildings

Approach

1. Using a viewfinder, focus on a section of David Hockney's *California Bank*.
2. Paint the squares and rectangles of the cartridge paper using a combination of chalk and oil pastels.
3. Place a variety of painted squares and rectangles overlapping on to the card.
4. Add some of the squares of material.
5. Glue the paper and fabric pieces to the card.
6. Arrange the fabric strips and the strips of coloured paper on top of the collage and glue them to the card.
7. If there are any spaces in between the blocks of colour, fill them in using the oil pastels.

Resources
- A5 card (15cm^2)
- Strips of coloured paper of varying widths
- Small squares and rectangles of cartridge paper
- Squares and strips of material
- Glue
- Scissors
- Chalk and oil pastels in blue, mauve, purple and pink
- Viewfinder (see page 19)

Landscape

3D Buildings

Approach

Resources
- A3 Sketch paper
- Sketch pencils
- Fine-line felt-tipped pens
- Oil pastels
- Glue
- Scissors
- A selection of boxes

1. As a starting point, look again at the sketches of buildings that have already been completed on page 15.
2. Enlarge the sketches on to the A3 paper and outline them with a fine-line felt-tipped pen.
3. Using the oil pastels, colour in the sketch to create a vibrant design.
4. Cut out sections and stick them to the sides of the boxes to create a colourful building.
5. Arrange a selection of black and white buildings and vibrantly coloured ones to create a dramatic and eye-catching display.

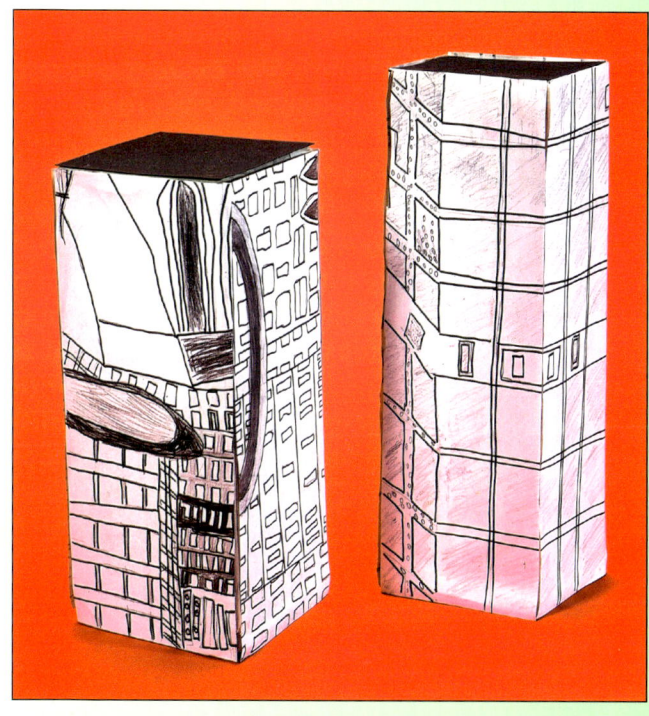

Michael Cruickshank (1957–)

View across The Sussex Weald by Michael Cruickshank (1957–), 2003 © Michael Cruickshank

Michael Cruickshank is an English landscape painter who works in oils, acrylics and watercolours. He studied Fine Art and Painting at Exeter College of Art, England, and graduated in 1980. His love of landscape stems from childhood visits to his grandmother in rural Lincolnshire. Michael now lives in Sussex, England, and uses a seventeenth-century timber-framed barn, which adjoins his home, as a gallery to exhibit his paintings.

In this painting, Michael uses the delicacy of watercolour to capture this typically English scene. The picture divides readily into foreground, middle ground and distance and this has been achieved by overlaying washes of transparent colour, adding the darker tones towards the end. The church in the middle distance provides not just a focal point to the painting but also an interesting contrast to what is essentially a view of pure landscape. Red roof tiles give a counterpoint to the greens of the surrounding foliage. Blues and blue-greens define the far distance, while the warm yellows and textures in the partly shaded stubble field complete the composition.

Landscape

Landscape Sketches

Resources
- Sketchbooks
- Pencils
- Camera
- Viewfinder

Approach

1. Look at Cruickshank's *View across The Sussex Weald* and discuss the features and objects included in the landscape.
2. Take a walk outside and look at the landscape. Choose a viewpoint that has an obvious foreground, middle ground and background.
3. Discuss the focal points of the view. What buildings are in the landscape? Where are they in relation to other features of the view?
4. Using a viewfinder, select a composition for the picture. Make sure the focal point is to the left or right of centre. Draw the outline of the landscape.
5. Add details to the drawing such as buildings and trees.
6. Look at the colours in the viewfinder. Using a soft pencil, number areas on the drawing and note the corresponding colours at the side of the picture.
7. Take a photograph of the view sketched.
8. Compare the finished sketch with the photograph back in the classroom.

Making a Viewfinder

Viewfinders enable the children to focus on a smaller portion of a view whilst drawing. Simple viewfinders can be made in advance of this activity using a square of card with a smaller square cut out from the middle.

Torn Paper Landscape

In *View across The Sussex Weald*, Michael Cruickshank gives the landscape more depth by using stronger tones and colours in the foreground with lighter ones in the background.

Resources
- A3 Sketch paper
- A4 Pale coloured card
- Red poster paint
- Brushes
- Scissors
- Glue

Approach

1. Divide the paper in to three equal sections.
2. Paint horizontal strokes across the top section with the darkest red for the foreground.
3. Paint the middle section with a slightly lighter red for the middle ground.
4. Paint the bottom section with the lightest red for the background. Leave to dry.
5. Cut out the three sections and tear in to small pieces.
6. Arrange the pieces on to the background card to show how three different tones create a sense of depth.
7. Glue the pieces on to the card.

Charcoal Pictures

Approach

1. Look again at the landscape photographs taken on the walk on page 19. Using a viewfinder, focus on a small section of landscape, for example part of a window, a door, stonework or brickwork.
2. Sketch the view using a charcoal stick.
3. Glue the picture on to a larger mount in a contrasting colour.

Resources
- Viewfinders (see page 19)
- Charcoal sticks
- Coloured card for mounting
- Sketch paper
- Glue
- Landscape photographs from page 19

Watercolour Landscape

Landscape

Resources
- Landscape photographs and sketches from page 19
- Watercolour paints
- Brushes
- A4 Sketch paper
- A3 Cardboard
- Masking tape
- Pencils

Approach

1. Look again at Cruickshank's *View across The Sussex Weald* and the landscape photographs taken from the activity on page 19. Discuss the composition of the pictures, reminding the children about the three sections needed in a landscape: foreground, middle ground and distance.
2. Lightly sketch the outline of the landscape on to the paper.
3. Stick the paper on to the cardboard using masking tape around the edges.

4. Apply a light colour wash to the sky area. Leave to dry.
5. Following the colour notes from the pencil sketch activity (page 19), use diluted colours to paint the background areas of the view. Do not saturate the paper.
6. Paint the rest of the picture, applying stronger tones to the foreground by building up layers of colour. When dry, carefully remove the masking tape.
7. Frame the paintings and set up a class exhibition with each picture labelled appropriately. Invite other classes to visit for the 'exhibition opening'. Encourage some children to act as guides.
8. Another idea is to scan the paintings into the computer and use them to make a selection of greetings cards.

Sculpture
Pablo Picasso (1881–1973)

The Owl, 1952 (mixed media) by Pablo Picasso (1881–1973) Hamburg Kunsthalle, Hamburg Germany/Bridgeman Art Library

Picasso was born in Spain. At the age of fourteen, Picasso and his family moved to Barcelona and he enrolled in the School of Fine Arts, where his father was a teacher. His extraordinary talent was soon recognised and by 1896 he had his first studio. After a few years, he moved to Paris, where he lived and worked for the rest of his life.

Picasso preferred his sculptures to his paintings and did not want to sell them. In his sculptures, Picasso displayed his originality and love of using everyday objects in his work. He often used 'found objects' in his sculptures such as used pieces of junk from scrap metal merchants, toy cars, nuts and bolts to create a dramatic effect. In this sculpture, *The Owl*, Picasso used mixed media such as clay and found objects.

Sculpture

Bird Outline

Picasso's love of animals is reflected in his work. He produced many sculptures of birds and his ideas always started from drawings. He would sketch the outline of a picture and then fill in the shapes and details with colour.

Resources
- Coloured paper for background
- White paper for drawing
- 3D stuffed birds or photographs of birds
- Black felt-tipped pen
- Scissors
- Pencils
- Glue

Approach

1. Look carefully at the photographs of real birds and talk about the shape of their beaks, legs and feet.
2. Using a pencil, create a line drawing of one of the birds.
3. Trace over the pencil outline with a black felt-tipped pen.
4. Cut out the bird shape and glue it on to the coloured paper.

Pastel Birds

Resources
- Black sugar paper
- White chalk pastels
- Silver pen
- Pencil
- Bird sketches from previous activity

Approach

1. Look again at Picasso's sculpture, *The Owl*, and discuss how Picasso has represented the features such as feathers, feet, eyes and beak.
2. Draw an outline of a bird from the previous activity on to a piece of black sugar paper using a pencil.
3. Trace the outline, using a silver pen.
4. Draw in the shapes to create the skeleton of the bird.
5. Using a white chalk pastel fill in the shapes in a Picasso style.

23

Modroc Owl Sculpture

Resources
- Modroc plaster bandages
- Newspaper
- Paintbrush
- Masking tape
- Poster paint in black and white
- A bowl of water

Approach

1. Look carefully at Picasso's *The Owl* and discuss how his use of black and white paint creates a dramatic image.
2. Scrunch up pieces of newspaper to form the bird shape.
3. Apply masking tape to hold the newspaper in shape.
4. Cut the modroc into strips.
5. Dip the strips of modroc in the water and attach them to the bird.
6. Smooth the modroc over the bird shape using the paintbrush. Allow the sculpture to dry.
7. Paint the sculpture white. Allow the paint to dry.
8. Using the black paint, create Picasso-like designs on the bird.

Bird Sculpture

Sculpture

Approach

1. Look again at Picasso's *The Owl* and photographs of birds. Discuss how the different features of a bird could be represented using a variety of modelling materials.
2. Using newspaper, roll and mould the paper into shape to create the main frame of the bird.
3. Bind the newspaper together using masking tape.
4. For the legs, use three pieces of thin wire and twist them together.
5. Feed the wire through the body of the bird, bending it down on both sides to form two legs.
6. Fan out the three strands at the bottom of the two ends of wire to create the claws of the bird.
7. Place the claws on a block of wood and attach using a strong stapler, in order to support the bird.
8. Using newspaper and PVA glue, papier-mâché the frame of the bird.
9. Add an extra layer of papier-mâché, using plain white paper, to strengthen the body.
10. Paint the bird, using poster paint mixed with sand.
11. Embellish the bird using a selection of found natural materials to create effect.
12. Give the sculpture a title.

Resources
- Poster paints mixed with sand and glue
- Paintbrushes
- PVA glue
- Newspaper
- Plain white paper
- Blocks of wood
- A selection of natural materials
- Thin wire
- Stapler
- Masking tape

Henry Moore (1898–1986)

Rocking Chair No.2 (bronze) by Henry Spencer Moore (1898–1986) Christie's Images, London, UK/Bridgeman Art Library

Henry Moore was born in Yorkshire, in the north of England. During his youth, he became fascinated by sculptures cut into stone which he frequently saw while he attended elementary school. His mother, Mary Baker, played an important role in the career of her young son and in 1941 he was appointed a member of the board of the Tate Gallery in London. In 1919, he joined the School of Fine Arts, but he found his real source of inspiration in the sculptures displayed in the British Museum, London. This is where he finally made the decision to become a sculptor.

In his sculpture, *Rocking Chair No. 2*, Henry Moore depicts a mother and child, one of his constant themes, holding hands. The mother is balancing the child on her knees in a playful position. The sculpture is made from bronze.

Live Model Sketches

Sculpture

Approach

1. Discuss different types of sculpture. Look at Moore's *Rocking Chair No. 2* and talk about the materials he has used and how the sculpture was made.

2. If possible, visit a museum to look at a variety of 3D sculptures and discuss what they represent. Are they human or an animal? What position are the figures in? Are they the same level?

3. Working in threes, two children act as models whilst the third directs the pair into a suitable pose for their pencil sketch. Ask the children to think about the following during their poses: high and low shapes, lying on the floor, one child standing up while the other poses in a lower position, the position of the arms and legs.

4. Ensure that the models always have two body parts joined at all times. Use a digital camera to photograph the children's poses.

5. Ask children who are not involved in the pose to sketch the basic outline of the shape, ensuring there is no detail in their sketch. Sketch three different poses on one sheet of paper and choose the best drawing.

6. Outline the sketches using fine-line black pens.

Resources
- A4 Cartridge paper
- Sketch pencils
- Picture of the Henry Moore sculpture
- Other 3D sculptures
- Fine-line black pen
- Two children acting as models
- Black card

Charcoal Sketches

Resources
- Initial sketches from page 27
- Charcoal
- A4 Cartridge paper
- Photographs of sculptures
- Red or black card

Approach

1. Using the initial pencil sketches from page 27, draw the chosen pose on to the cartridge paper using the charcoal.
2. Ensure there are no gaps in the sketch and that all parts are joined.
3. Use a finger to smudge gently the inside of the sketch to create a shadow.
4. The background must stay pure white.
5. Rub the charcoal in towards the centre of the body to create highlights, a sense of depth and the initial stages of a 3D sculpture.

Modroc Sculptures

Resources
- Modroc plaster bandages
- Newspaper
- Paintbrush
- Masking tape
- Black and white poster paint
- A bowl of water

Approach

1. Look at Henry Moore's sculpture and discuss its simple but effective form.
2. Scrunch up pieces of newspaper to form the shape of a seated person.
3. Bind the shape with masking tape.
4. Cut the modroc in to strips and dip the strips in to the water.
5. Smooth the modroc over the person shape using the paintbrush. Let the sculpture dry.
6. Mix the black and white paint to get a grey colour.
7. Paint the sculpture.

Clay Sculpture

Sculpture

Children should have plenty of practice with the clay before beginning a sculpture. Demonstrate how to mould and shape the clay so that they have a clear idea of how to use it. Use words such as pinch, squeeze, roll, scrunch and twist, allowing the children to practise shaping and moulding the piece of clay. Use the clay to make a variety of shapes, for example a long shape, a sausage shape, a flat shape, a cube shape, cuboids and spherical shapes.

Resources
- One piece of clay per child
- Cutting tools
- Clay boards
- Water spray
- Initial pencil sketches from page 27
- PVA glue
- Paint

Approach

1. Give each child a piece of clay. Manipulate the clay in the hands to soften it.
2. Begin to shape the clay in to a block that is approximately the same shape as the original sketch (see page 27), for example a tall cuboid, a long cuboid, a cube or a sphere.
3. Using the clay tool, begin to trim the clay to form the basic shape of the pose, reminding the children to keep strong lines with no breaks.
4. Use a water spray to keep the clay wet so that it is easy to work with.
5. Use hands to shape, mould and smooth the final sculpture.
6. Paint and varnish with PVA glue to give it shine.

Imagination

Raymond Briggs (1934–)

Extract from *THE BEAR* by Raymond Briggs, published by Jonathan Cape. Used by permission of The Random House Group Limited

Raymond Briggs was educated at Rutlish School in London, England. At the age of fifteen, he attended the Wimbledon School of Art, where he studied painting for four years. It was during this time that he became convinced that he wanted to be an illustrator. He was soon earning a living illustrating picture books and teaching at Brighton College of Art. He has won many major awards and has written a succession of very popular books for both adults and children. His most famous book, *The Snowman*, has been made into a film. Raymond Briggs now lives in Sussex, England.

In his book, *The Bear*, the final illustrations show a very simple style, which creates a focal point in each image. The changing colours depict the passing of time in the story and the images show progression as the Bear travels from land to sea. The ending of the story is told purely through Raymond Briggs' wonderful illustrations with no text.

Bear Sketches

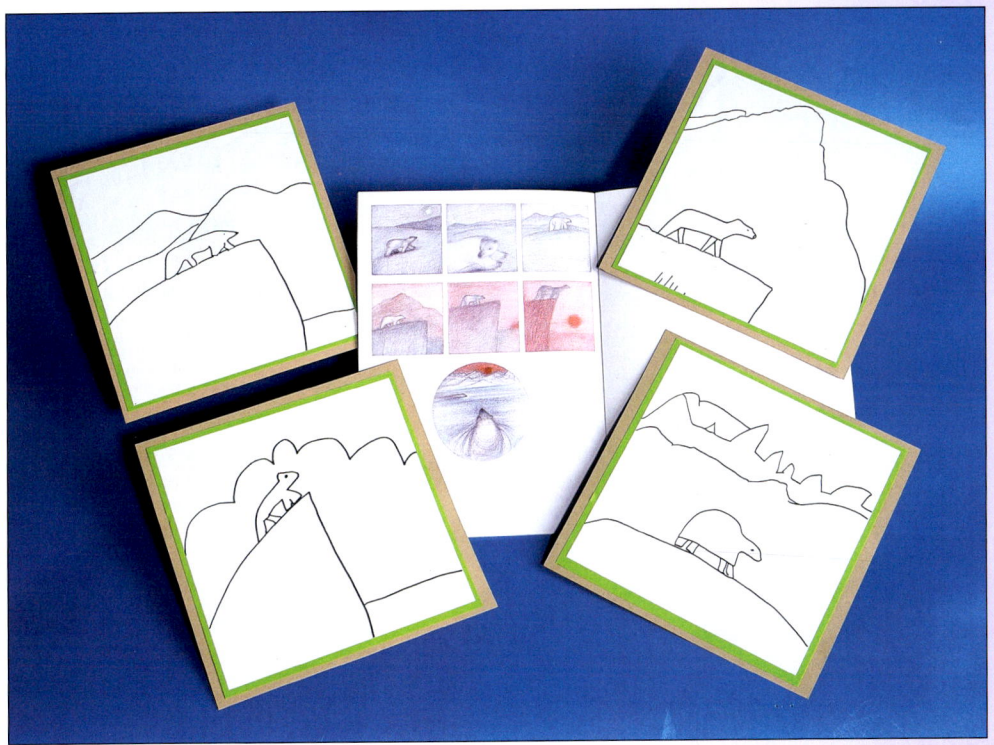

Imagination

Resources
- A4 Sketch paper
- Sketch pencils

Approach

1. Read the story, *The Bear*, and ask the children to explain what is happening in the sequence of illustrations on the last page.
2. Comment on how Briggs uses the images to tell a story without text.
3. Choose one of the images from the page and create a simple line drawing, using basic shapes and outlines only.

Powder Paints

Approach

1. Enlarge the original pencil sketches to A3 size.
2. Trim the cardboard to match the shape of Raymond Briggs' illustrations.
3. Look carefully at the colours and tones in Raymond Briggs' illustrations and discuss how they tell us about the passing of time in the story.
4. Using masking tape, attach the sketches to the red card.
5. Using powder paints, develop the sketches into paintings and match the colours and tones to Raymond Briggs' images. When the painting is finished, carefully remove the masking tape and mount.

Resources
- A3 White card
- Powder paints
- Sketch pencil
- Paintbrushes
- A3 Red card
- Masking tape

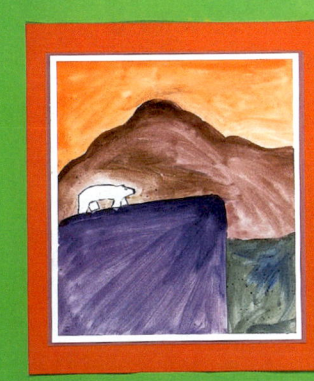  

31

A Storyboard in Colour

Resources
- Picture books
- A3 Sketch paper
- A2 White card
- Sketch pencil
- Coloured pencils
- Masking tape
- A4 Blue card
- Glue
- Scissors

Swirling Seascape

Approach

1. Look again at Briggs' illustrations. Discuss how landscapes like the one in *The Bear* could be created using different art materials.
2. Using masking tape, fix the sketch paper to the card.
3. Mix the paint with the glue to thicken it.
4. Mix the sand with the blue paint to give it texture.
5. Using a sketch pencil, draw the waves with strong, directional strokes.
6. Paint the sketch using swirling brushstrokes to create a sea effect.
7. Add glitter glue to emphasise movement and texture. Remove the masking tape carefully when dry.

Resources
- Glitter glue
- A4 White card
- A5 Sketch paper
- PVA glue
- Paintbrushes
- Sketch pencils
- Masking tape
- Poster paint in white and blue
- Sand

Approach

1. Look at other picture books and discuss the different styles of illustration. As a class, choose a favourite storybook – the example on this page is from the well-known story *Jonah and the Whale*.

2. Read the book. Make a concise list of the six main events in order on a whiteboard. Divide a piece of A3 sketch paper into six equal sections.

3. Produce a storyboard using Raymond Briggs' style. Begin by drawing a basic pencil outline for each of the main events.

4. Cut out each image. Using masking tape on the back of each section, attach each image to a piece of card 'storyboard'. Add detail and texture to each image using coloured pencils. Experiment with Briggs' style of lines and shading. Mount each image on to blue card.

5. Finally, stick the completed images, in the right order, on to the piece of white card 'storyboard', leaving a space between each one. Compare the children's storyboards with *The Bear* illustrations.

Story Scene

Imagination

Approach

1. Create a fabric collage using Raymond Briggs' final circular image from *The Bear* as a starting point.

2. Re-read the favourite story from page 32 and decide as a class which scene to produce as a circular collage. The example on this page shows the whale from *Jonah and the Whale*.

3. Discuss with the children which fabrics to use for the different sections of the collage. Make a rough sketch of their ideas on the whiteboard.

4. Draw a circle on to the hessian, making sure to leave a border around the sides.

5. Draw the outline of the image on to the fabric in pencil, showing the different sections of the picture, for example the sky, the mountains, the sea and the figure in the foreground.

6. Select and cut the fabrics needed for the different sections to the appropriate size. The fabric collage could be worked on using small groups of children focusing on one section at a time.

7. Create texture by overlapping, layering, folding and scrunching the fabrics.

8. Attach the pieces of fabric on to the circle of hessian, using a variety of threads and glue.

9. Fix the characters and objects to the collage (made from fabric stuffed with wadding) with glue.

10. Embellish the design with sequins and beads.

Resources

- Large piece of hessian (1m²)
- Small pieces of fabric in an assortment of shapes and contrasting textures, e.g. silk, muslin, cotton, jute, scrim, strips of ribbon and linen
- Beads, glass beads and sequins
- Wadding
- A selection of threads, e.g. cotton, embroidery, wool and ribbon
- Tapestry and large-eyed needles
- Scissors
- Glue
- Sketch pencils
- Picture book from previous activity (page 32)

Containers and Objects

Kate Malone (1959–)

Choir Boy and Choir Girl Pineapple, 1993, (Stoneware, height 18cm) by Kate Malone © Kate Malone

Kate Malone went to school in Herefordshire, England, where at fourteen she discovered the Ceramics Department. She has a first-class honours degree in Ceramics and studied at the Royal College of Art in London where she received her MA. She is best known for her bold, sculptural ceramics in the form of pumpkins and pineapples. Her colourful pots, fruit forms and sea creatures are well known throughout the world and she has been commissioned by many architects, including several outside the UK.

Kate Malone's work is very distinctive and reflects a sense of fun. Her pineapple pots symbolise hospitality and prosperity. For her, containers or vessels stand for protection, shelter and preservation. The colours she uses in her work also have a meaning. In the pineapple pot, the oranges and yellows stand for splendour and happiness, whereas the greens stand for youth and confidence. Kate Malone says, 'The patterns of the different varieties of real pineapples are fascinating, the fruit smells so sensual when ripe, it tastes like no other … the fact that fruits are sorts of packages that hold juice-liquid – just like a pot does – also make it logical to make a pot like a pineapple … the sheer shape just lends itself perfectly.'

Containers and Objects

Chalk Pastels

Resources
- A selection of fruit and vegetables
- A4 Cartridge paper
- Sketch pencils
- Chalk pastels
- Tissue paper (green) cut into leaf shapes
- Pipe cleaners cut into small sections

Approach

1. Look at Kate Malone's *Choir Boy and Choir Girl Pineapple* and talk about how she uses fruit as a source of inspiration in her work.
2. Arrange a selection of fruit and vegetables to create a composition for a still life painting.
3. Discuss the composition in terms of colour, shape, texture and pattern.
4. Look carefully at the composition and choose a viewpoint.
5. Draw the still life composition, making sure it fills the whole page.
6. Using chalk pastels, add colour to create a vibrant image.
7. Stick on pipe cleaners as stalks for the fruit.
8. Use the tissue paper leaf shapes to decorate the final image.

Papier-Mâché Pineapples

Resources
- 1 litre plastic soft drinks bottles
- PVA glue
- Newspaper
- Green card
- Poster paint
- Paintbrushes

Approach

1. Use the lower portion of the plastic bottle as the base for the pineapple shape and coat it with PVA glue.
2. Using strips of newspaper, covered with the glue, build up layers on the bottle to form the basic shape (paper can be scrunched up or rolled to create extra padding).
3. After the shape is dry, scrunch up small pieces of newspaper to create the prickly texture of the pineapple skin.
4. Cover the whole container with at least another two layers of papier-mâché.
5. Allow to dry, and then paint with poster paint.
6. Cut the green card in to the shape of the pineapple leaves and stick to the inside rim of the pot.
7. Try making other 3D fruit pots using the same technique. Some could have lids made from papier-mâché and decorated with card stalks and leaves.

Pot Design

Much of Kate Malone's work has a special symbolism or meaning. She particularly likes the jug shape as it reminds her of friendship and sharing. She thinks that jugs make you feel safe and that wonderful things will pour out of them. Kate Malone says, 'When I heard that a pineapple is traditionally a symbol of hospitality, it really reinforced the strength of the image and I have made possibly some twenty pineapples since, ranging in size from small enough to hold in the palm of your hand to big enough for a child to climb inside.'

Resources
- A collection of functional and decorative pots
- A selection of fruit and vegetables
- Photographs of fruit and vegetables
- A3 Cartridge paper
- Sketch pencils
- Oil pastels
- Glue
- Tissue paper

Approach

1. Look again at Malone's *Choir Boy and Choir Girl Pineapple* and compare these with a class collection of pots and containers on display. Discuss their effectiveness in terms of function and appearance.

2. Look carefully at the individual designs in terms of shape, form, space and pattern.

3. Encourage the children to design their own pots, using a fruit or vegetable as a source of inspiration. Ensure that the children have time to examine a collection of real fruit and vegetables before making their decision. Discuss what each container might hold.

4. Sketch the design for a pot or other container on to A3 paper, starting with a basic fruit shape. Ensure the sketch fills most of the page.

5. Create a vibrant image by adding colour using oil pastels.

6. Cut out the pot design and mount it on to a colourful background.

7. Add a 3D element to the design, by attaching tissue paper leaves and stalks.

8. Give the pot or container a title.

Containers and Objects

Pineapple Clay Containers

Kate Malone's pots are made by a combination of press moulding and coiling; the main body is pressed, the top curvy lips are coiled. For the press moulding she uses a two-part plaster mould to create the basic form. For the coiling, she makes large ropes of clay and joins them together to make huge pots. Sometimes she adds chopped-up pieces of newspaper to the clay to stop it from cracking. She emphasises that the base of the pot is crucial and needs to be very strong. Kate Malone says, 'I was instinctively drawn to the pineapple form by the sheer beauty of the fruit itself; it has the crown of leaves at the top that really lift upwards in a rejoicing motion, the fruit surface is so complex and interesting and lends itself well to inspiring a surface of soft squidgy clay.'

Resources
- Clay (air hardening)
- Wooden base
- Clay tools
- Poster paints
- Paintbrushes
- Plastic bags

Approach

1. Look at Malone's pots and discuss them in terms of texture, shape, space and colour.
2. Use the wooden base to work on and roll out the slab of clay into a flat, circular base.
3. Roll the clay into strips to form coils.
4. Build up the sides of the container by laying coils around the edge of the base, one on top of another.
5. Using a clay tool, score the edges of the coiled clay before placing another coil on top.
6. Apply a mixture of water and clay before blending with fingers to make sure that the clay sticks together.
7. Create the pineapple shape by making the coils larger or smaller as needed.
8. Put the completed pot shape into an airtight, plastic bag to keep moist.
9. Create the surface texture of the pineapple by rolling up small pieces of clay to form ball shapes.
10. Using the clay tool, score the main pot and the ball shapes and apply them to the surface of the pot.
11. Blend in the ball shapes with the main pot shape using fingers.
12. Cut out leaf shapes and blend into the top of the pot by scoring and moistening.
13. Layer the leaf shapes to create the desired effect.
14. Score into the clay any details that are needed. Leave to dry naturally.
15. Paint the containers using poster paints in bright, bold colours.

Paul Cézanne (1839–1906)

The Black Marble Clock, c.1870 (oil on canvas) by Paul Cézanne (1839–1906) Private Collection/Bridgeman Art Library

Cézanne was born in the south of France. He studied Law from 1859 to 1861, but at the same time he attended drawing classes. In 1861, he decided to take up painting full time, having received a large inheritance on which he could live comfortably. He worked with the artist Camille Pissarro in the early 1870s and got to know and exhibit with other Impressionist artists. He is thought of today as the creator of the era of modern art. Later on in life, he became interested in still life paintings and his influence on twentieth-century art is considerable.

In his painting, *The Black Marble Clock*, Cézanne has placed together a selection of natural and manufactured objects to form a dramatic image. The open natural form of the shell against the cold marble of the clock is striking. The contrasting colours in the painting, such as the white of the tablecloth and the black of the clock, create a dramatic image. Cézanne has not given the clock face any hands and this portrays a sense of timelessness, which somehow makes the painting even more beguiling.

Containers and Objects

Multimedia Still Life Painting

Resources
- Squares of cardboard
- Poster paints
- PVA glue
- Plasticine
- White card
- Scissors
- Strips of black and turquoise card
- Paintbrushes
- Sketch pencil
- Tissue paper cut into small pieces

Approach

1. Look at the effect of light and shade and the texture of the objects in Cézanne's painting, *The Black Marble Clock*.
2. Focus on the cup, saucer and the vase and sketch them on a square piece of cardboard.
3. Paint the background red.
4. Using small pieces of plasticine, build up the cup and saucer shape to create a 3D effect.
5. Attach pieces of tissue paper to the cup and saucer by painting them on with PVA glue. Allow to dry and harden.
6. Paint the cup and saucer using contrasting colours.
7. Using the outline of the vase as a starting point, cut out its basic shape in white card and stick it on.
8. Decorate with the strips of black and turquoise card.
9. Paint the foreground using thick, swirling brush strokes to give the effect of the draped tablecloth.
10. Choose any other two objects from Cézanne's still life painting to make a different composition.

39

Still Life Composition

Resources
- Poster paints
- Digital camera
- Sketch pencil
- Paintbrushes (thick and fine)
- Sand
- Masking tape
- Cardboard
- Everyday objects
- A4 White card

Approach

1. Look again at Cézanne's painting *The Black Marble Clock*, and talk about the objects in the picture. Ask the children for ideas of everyday objects to include in a still life painting. Collect these objects together.
2. Create a composition for a still life using any two objects from Cézanne's painting, and two new objects.
3. Arrange the objects to form a still life. Take a photograph of the composition.
4. Sketch the composition on to a piece of card.
5. Attach the card to the cardboard base by placing masking tape around the edges of the card.
6. Using bright, contrasting colours, paint the sketch, starting from the background and working towards the foreground.
7. A small amount of sand could be mixed with the paint to create added texture.
8. Remove the masking tape when dry. Display the paintings with the photographs.

Containers and Objects

3D Clocks

Approach

1. For the clock face, cut out a circle from the white card, using a pair of compasses. Write in the numbers on the clock face with a fine-line black felt-tipped pen.

2. Cut out two strips of black card, one long and one short, for each hand of the clock. Draw an arrow on each hand using a gold pen. Place one end over the other and attach to the centre of the clock face using a split pin to hold them in place.

3. Cut out a square of cardboard that is slightly larger than the clock face. Paint it blue and allow to dry. Stick the clock face on to the blue cardboard base with PVA glue.

4. Cut out two thin strips of cardboard and stick one on each side of the cardboard clock base. Paint the cardboard strips red. Embellish the strips by placing two small pieces of cardboard on either end and paint them blue.

5. Paint two wooden craft sticks with the gold pen and place one on each of the cardboard strips.

6. Paint several of the wooden craft sticks red and stick them together to form a pyramid shape using a hot glue gun. Attach them to the lower section of the clock base and decorate the clock base with the gold pen.

7. Cut a thick strip of strong cardboard and fold it in half. Using a hot glue gun, stick the upper half of the cardboard strip to the back of the clock. Make sure that the lower half of the cardboard strip is resting on the display surface.

8. Glue a wooden craft stick to each end of the cardboard strip to give extra support.

Resources
- White card
- Pair of compasses
- Black fine-line felt-tipped pen
- Wooden craft sticks
- Gold pen
- Black card
- Split pins
- Poster paints (red and blue)
- Paintbrushes
- Glue gun
- Cardboard
- PVA glue
- Scissors

Pierre-Auguste Renoir (1841–1919)

Woman Playing the Guitar by Pierre-Auguste Renoir (1841–1919) © Corel

Pierre-Auguste Renoir was born in Limoges in France. In 1844 Renoir and his family moved to Paris, where his father earned his living as a tailor. Renoir left school in 1854 to begin an apprenticeship as a porcelain painter. He formed a lasting friendship with the artist Claude Monet, whom he worked with as a member of a group of Impressionists. He began to achieve success as a portrait artist in the late 1870s. The subject matter that inspired him most from the mid 1880s was that of women and children. He is among the most widely known and best-loved European painters.

In Renoir's painting, *Woman Playing the Guitar*, a young woman appears absorbed in playing her guitar. She seems very studious, but at the same time looks relaxed. She is sitting in a very comfortable chair and is resting her right foot on a cushion. The details in her dress match closely with the orangey gold tones of her guitar. The colours blend together to create a very harmonious image.

Containers and Objects

Guitar and Violin Sketches

Approach

1. Look at Renoir's painting, *Woman Playing the Guitar*. Compare the guitar in the picture to a real guitar.
2. Compare the guitar and the violin. Discuss them both in terms of shape and design.
3. Study the proportions of both instruments, such as the length of the handle compared with the body. Look carefully at the positioning of the circular hole and the strings.
4. Using the sketchbooks, produce a quick drawing of the outline of the guitar or violin with a focus on the overall shape. Do a second, more detailed sketch including the strings.
5. Place the guitar or violin on a stand and sketch it from an interesting angle.
6. Using the initial sketches as a starting point, as well as the instruments, draw a detailed sketch of one of them on the sketch paper.
7. Cut out the sketches and display them together with the instruments.

Resources
- Sketchbook
- A4 Sketch paper
- Sketch pencils
- A guitar
- A violin

43

Pastel and Watercolour Instruments

Resources
- A4 White and dusky pink card
- Chalk pastels
- Watercolours
- Paintbrushes
- Sketch pencils
- A guitar
- A violin
- Craft sticks in 2.5cm lengths
- Glue gun
- Scissors
- PVA glue

Approach

1. Place the guitar or violin on a stand at an interesting angle.
2. Choose one of the instruments and produce a simple sketch of the outline.
3. Fill in the details such as the strings and the handle with a focus on getting the proportions right.
4. Look at the colours of the instruments and focus on the darker and lighter tones of colour. Choose a combination of chalk pastels and watercolour paints to work with. Using diluted watercolours, paint the sketches. Apply stronger tones to match the darker sections. Use the chalk pastels to highlight the brighter tones.
5. Cut out the painted sketches and draw around an outline of the shape on the pink card with a sketch pencil.
6. Cut out the outline on the pink card.
7. Using the glue gun, stick four craft sticks to the back of the painted guitar or violin shapes.
8. Using the glue gun, stick the other end of the craft sticks to the matching unpainted shape on the pink card to create a 3D effect.
9. Make sure the painted section is displayed on top of the unpainted one.

Containers and Objects

3D Guitar

Resources
- Cardboard
- Red corrugated cardboard
- String
- Craft sticks 5cm lengths
- Gold pen
- Black poster paint
- Paintbrushes
- Glue gun
- Craft knife
- Sketch pencil

Approach

1. Look again at Renoir's painting and brainstorm different ideas for constructing a 3D guitar model.
2. Cut out two identical guitar body shapes from the cardboard.
3. Draw a circle on one of the guitar shapes and cut it out using a craft knife. Keep this shape for the front section of the guitar.
4. Outline the shape using a gold pen.
5. Paint another thicker line around the outside of both cardboard guitars, using black poster paint.
6. Place the front section of the guitar slightly to one side over the lower one, to give a more 3D effect.
7. Using a glue gun, attach the craft sticks so that one end is on each cardboard guitar to create a 3D effect.
8. Cut out a rectangular shape from the cardboard to use as a guitar handle.
9. Using the glue gun, stick red corrugated cardboard over the handle to add colour. Attach the handle to the inside of the front section of the guitar.
10. For the top section of the guitar handle, cut out a small piece of card and glue it on to the top of the handle at a slight angle. Attach three wooden craft sticks to this section of the handle.
11. Using a glue gun, stick a pyramid of craft sticks at the base of the front section of the guitar.
12. Cut six lengths of string and glue one end to the craft sticks on the guitar's handle and the other to the pyramid of craft sticks at the base of the guitar. Make sure the strings are taut.
13. Display the models with real guitars and the Renoir picture.

Portrait

Pablo Picasso (1881–1973)

Portrait of Dora Maar, 1937 by Pablo Picasso (1881–1973) Musee Picasso, Paris France/ Bridgeman Art Library © Succession Picasso/ DACS 2003

Pablo Picasso was born in Spain where his father taught painting and recognised his son's artistic abilities from an early age. In 1904, Picasso moved to Paris, where he rented a studio in the famous Montmartre area. His work progressed through very different stages, such as his Blue and Rose periods, Cubism, Sculpture and Ceramics. He is as famous for his sculptures as he is for his paintings. Later on in life, he became interested in ceramics and made decorative pots, plates and containers, often shaped into figures and faces.

In this painting, *Portrait of Dora Maar*, we see an image of a beautiful young woman. The painting is in an experimental style and shows both front and profile view of her face. The eyes are different colours and Picasso has painted the portrait in bright, vibrant tones. The background of the painting, which appears to be like an enclosed box, gives the impression of Dora Maar being trapped and confined. Dora Maar was a photographer and enjoyed discussing Picasso's paintings with him. He decided to paint her because they had become very close and Picasso liked to use the people who were important to him as his models.

Oil Pastel Portraits

Portrait

Resources
- A4 Cartridge paper
- Sketch pencils
- Oil pastels

Approach

1. In Picasso's portrait of Dora Maar, her eyes are at different angles. It is as if Picasso looked at her from two different viewpoints and created one image.

2. Look carefully at the portrait and discuss with the children how he has used the vibrant colours to create such a striking image.

3. Discuss how Picasso has painted Dora Maar's hair using blues, greens, reds and blacks.

4. Sketch the portrait, making sure to include the enclosed box-like background.

5. Add vibrant colour to the portrait with a selection of oil pastels.

Self-Portraits

Picasso believed that children have a gift for expressing their ideas in paintings. This explains why children produce such individual paintings. He said, 'When I was as old as these children, I could draw like Raphael but it took me a lifetime to learn to draw like them.' – Picasso.

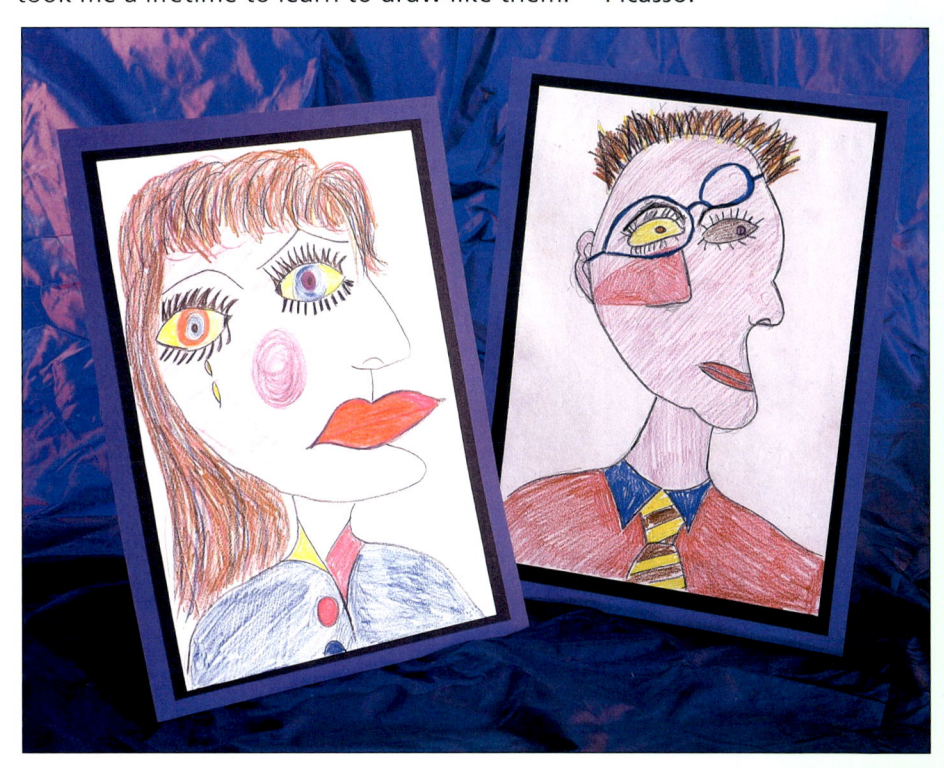

Resources
- A4 Cartridge paper
- Sketch pencils
- Bright colouring pencils
- Digital camera
- Children's photographs

Approach

1. Take a photograph of the children's faces using a digital camera if possible.

2. Using the photograph as a starting point, sketch a self-portrait in Picasso's style.

3. Add colour to the image using colouring pencils.

3D Self-Portraits

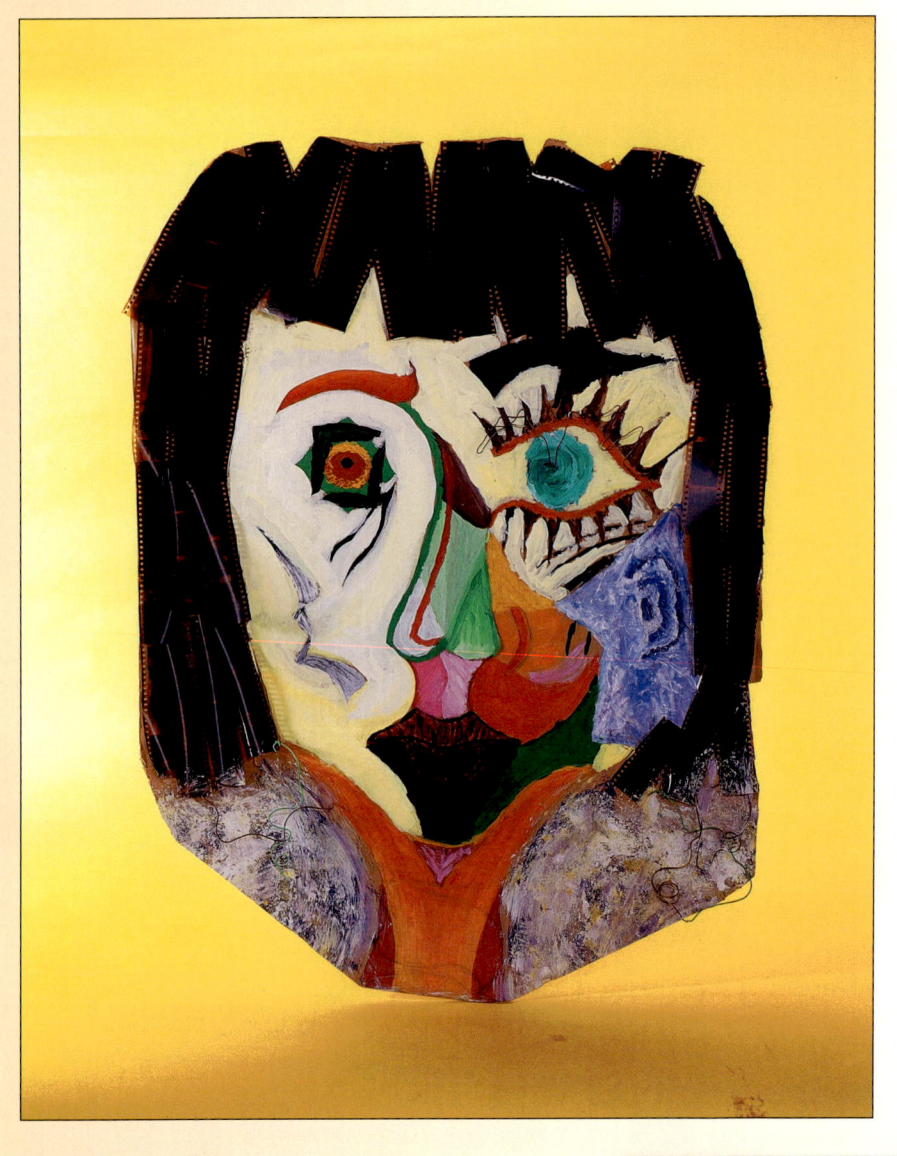

Resources
- Poster paints
- Paintbrushes
- Wool in a variety of colours
- A selection of manufactured materials such as buttons, sequins, pipe cleaners and wire
- Photograph negatives
- Sketch pencils
- Thick cardboard
- PVA glue

Approach

1. Draw the outline of a face on a large piece of cardboard and fill in the features.

2. Talk about colours that reflect different moods such as blue for sadness and yellow for happiness. Discuss favourite colours and use them to paint the 3D portrait to reflect the mood of the individual.

3. Use a selection of materials for the hair to create texture, for example different colours of wool, pipe cleaners or even photograph negatives and stick on using the glue.

4. Make the eyes look dramatic by painting them in bright colours.

5. Using glue, stick on other materials such as wire for eyelashes and buttons or sequins.

3D Portraits

Portrait

Picasso was constantly willing to change his painting technique and enjoyed experimenting with different approaches. He said, 'There are, of course, great painters who have a certain style. However, I always thrash about rather wildly. I am a bit of a tramp. You can see me at this moment, but I have already changed, I am already somewhere else. I can never be tied down, and that is why I have no style.' – Picasso

Resources
- PVA glue
- Poster paints
- Paintbrushes
- Thick cardboard
- Scissors
- Sketch pencils
- Card

Approach

1. Draw the outline shape of Dora Maar's face on a large piece of cardboard. Cut out the shape and use it as a base.

2. Score vertically down the middle of the base so that it bends easily.

3. Cut out two strips of card and attach to the back of the base to hold it in place.

4. Draw another outline shape of the face and divide it into three sections. Cut out the sections.

5. Look carefully at the colours in Dora Maar's portrait and using a sketch pencil divide the individual sections into blocks of different colours.

6. Paint the sections using vibrant colours to reflect the colours in Picasso's portrait.

7. Using a smaller piece of card, draw three shapes for each of the eyes and two for the mouth. Cut out the shapes and paint them different colours.

8. Attach the shapes by sticking them on in layers to represent the eyes.

9. Attach the mouth shapes by placing them in the correct position.

10. Arrange the sections on to the base, making sure that some of the sections overlap to create depth.

11. Attach the sections to the base with glue. Hang the portrait to display.

Daphne Todd (1947–)

Ron and Ray Pett, Butchers, (50×40 ins oil on panel) by Daphne Todd (1947–)
© Daphne Todd

Daphne Todd was born in Yorkshire and grew up in Kent, England. She studied at the Slade School of Fine Art and, while there, won awards for drawing, landscape painting and figurative painting. She taught Art part-time in the 1970s and became Director of Studies at Heatherly School of Art. In 1994, Daphne became the first female president of the Royal Society of Portrait Painters and was awarded the OBE in 2002. She has won several major prizes and her work is exhibited in the National Portrait Gallery, the Royal Academy, Cambridge University, Oxford University, the Royal Collection and many other institutions and Private Collections throughout Britain and Europe.

In this painting, Daphne Todd has created a double portrait of Ron and Ray Pett, who are cousins and work together in a family-run butcher's shop. This oil painting was produced over several weeks, after working hours, in the back room of the shop, where the meat was kept. A combination of hot and cold light has been used – the yellow light is warm and the blue light is cold. Daphne says, 'Be absolutely sure what the lightest part in your painting is before you start. In this painting, the bit of strip lighting remains lighter than any part of the white coats. So you cannot simply use white paint for them!'

In the painting there are many clues about the sort of work the two men do. For example, the dead turkeys, the butchers' knives, the wooden table in the foreground and the meat hooks in the background. Daphne says, 'When you are composing a picture with lots of things in it, be aware of the shapes of the spaces between them.'

Oil Pastel Portraits

Portrait

Resources
- A4 Sketch paper
- Sketch pencils
- Masking tape
- Large pieces of cardboard as a base
- Oil pastels
- Photographs/portraits of other people in a work setting

Approach

1. In Daphne Todd's painting *Ron and Ray Pett, Butchers*, there are many clues about what the two men do for a living, such as the turkeys hanging in the background, the apron that one of them is wearing and their white coats. Discuss the painting with the children and talk about it in terms of composition, for example the different poses of the two men – one is bending over and the other is standing upright with his hands resting on the wooden table with a turkey placed between them in the background.

2. Look at photographs of other portraits and discuss the clues that show what the people in them do for a living.

3. Place the sketch paper on a cardboard base and fix around the edges with masking tape.

4. Using the portrait of *Ron and Ray Pett, Butchers* as a starting point, sketch a portrait that depicts somebody in a job. Encourage the children to place clues in their pictures hinting at the work of the portrait sitter.

5. Using oil pastels, create a vibrant image. Focus the children to include the different facial expressions of the person in the portrait. Remove the masking tape carefully when the portrait is finished.

51

Still Life Painting

Daphne Todd says about her portraits, 'It is like a time capsule. It is for posterity … If you keep the portraits, you will find that your young self has sent a message to your older self and it will record more than you now realise because lots of things will have changed.'

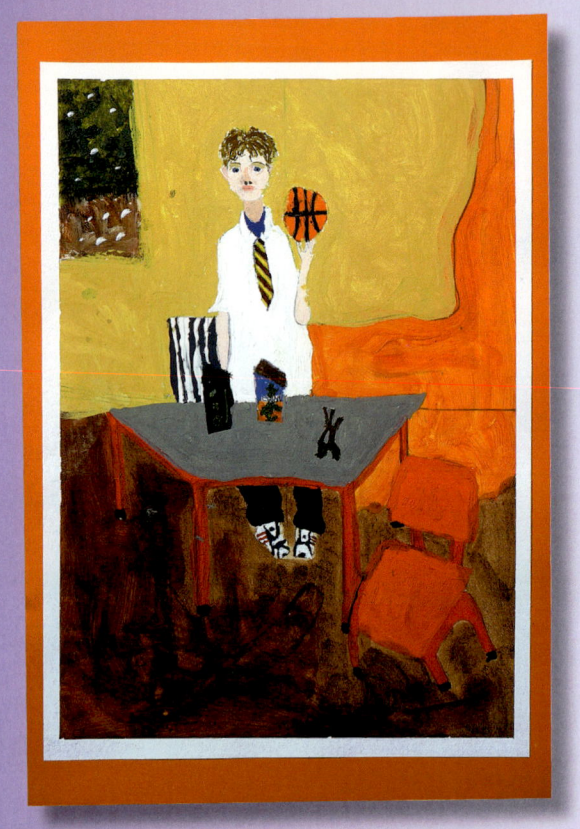

Resources
- A4 White card
- Sketch pencils
- Acrylic paints
- Masking tape
- Large pieces of cardboard as a base
- Paintbrushes
- Digital camera

Approach

1. Ask the children to bring in their favourite things such as books and games.
2. Create an effective composition comprising one child at a time.
3. Decide on a pose and take a photograph using a digital camera if possible.
4. Give the children their photograph to work from.
5. Using the masking tape, attach the white card to the cardboard base.
6. Using the photograph as a starting point, sketch the composition including the sitter's favourite things. Discuss how to paint a portrait.
7. Paint the sketches using acrylics. When dry, remove the masking tape and mount.
8. Look at the finished portraits and discuss the clues given in each picture about the sitter.

- Draw the shape of the face and divide it into four equal sections. Do not use a ruler.
- Draw the eyes on the horizontal line, the top of the eyes should be in line with the top of the ears.
- Draw the hair last making sure it follows the shape of the head.
- Paint the features of the face first and then the skin, look at the skin tone and how the colour of the skin varies, it is not one flat colour. Lastly paint the hair and once again look at the various tones of the hair.

Portrait

Modelling Dough and Tissue Paper Portraits

In her portraits, Daphne Todd likes to focus on a facial feature that perhaps stands out as being a bit different. She says, 'You need to go for something that strikes you as being particularly unusual – a very pointed nose, for example, or hooded eyes or a short upper lip …'.

Resources
- Modelling dough
- Tissue paper (white)
- PVA glue
- Poster paints
- Paintbrushes
- Scissors

Approach

1. Working in pairs, ask the children to look carefully at each other's face. Focus on the main features such as eyes, nose and mouth.
2. Create the basic shape of the face using the modelling dough.
3. Build up the features of the face by adding extra pieces of the dough.
4. Make sure the centres of the eyes protrude more than the edges to create the ball and socket effect.
5. Use thin strips of dough for the hair and place on top of the doughface.
6. Mix the PVA glue with water (two parts glue with one part water).
7. Cut the tissue paper into small squares.
8. Dip the tissue paper in to the glue mixture and place on the surface of the doughface and hair. Allow to dry.
9. Paint the dough portraits using poster paints. Leave to dry.
10. Paint the hair and the faces with PVA glue to give a shiny finish.

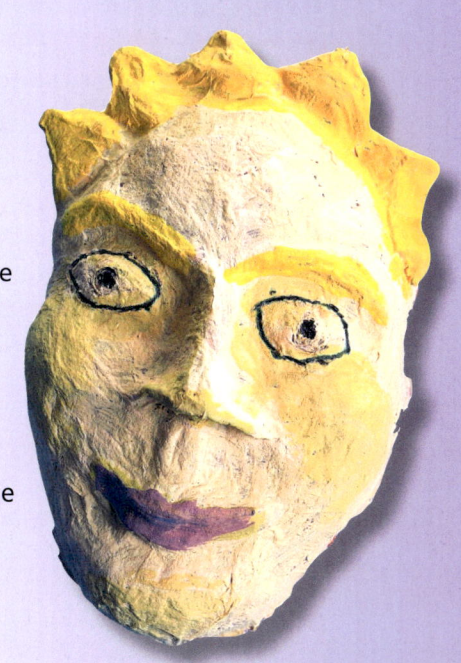

Nature

Henri Matisse (1869–1954)

Seville Still Life, 1910 (oil on canvas) by Henri Matisse (1869–1954) Hermitage, St Petersburg, Russia/Bridgeman Art Library
© Succession H Matisse/DACS 2003

Henri Matisse was born in France in 1869. In 1891, he moved to Paris to study contemporary art but he was particularly drawn to the Impressionists. He was influenced by the French painters Paul Cézanne and Paul Gauguin and also by Vincent Van Gogh. From the 1920s until his death, Matisse spent most of his time in the south of France and especially in Nice. It was there that he painted local scenes with a thin, fluid application of very bright colours. Unlike many artists, he became internationally famous during his lifetime and earned the name, 'Master of Colour'.

In Matisse's *Seville Still Life* painting, the background provides a rich contrast in terms of colour and design to the rest of the composition. Its deep, rich colour creates a dramatic image. The focal point of the painting is the potted plant, which appears simpler than its decorative textile setting.

Still Life Pastels

Nature

Resources
- A selection of potted plants
- A4 Sketch paper
- Chalk and oil pastels
- Sketch pencils

Approach

1. Look carefully at Matisse's *Seville Still Life* painting. Talk about how the eye is drawn to the potted plant because it is a living thing in the midst of designer fabric. Focus on the line, shape and colour of the plant.

2. Using a pencil, make a careful sketch of a plant, putting in as much detail as possible.

3. Using a combination of chalk and oil pastels, add colour to the sketch.

4. Alternatively, cut out the individual sketches and display in a 3D vase made from shiny paper.

Pastel Leaf Design

Resources
- A4 Sketch paper
- Oil pastels
- Viewfinder 4cm^2
- Squares of sketch paper 20cm^2
- Sketch pencils
- Ruler

Approach

1. Matisse draws on nature for inspiration in his paintings and we can see this influence in *Seville Still Life*.

2. Ask the children to focus on the leaves in Matisse's painting and produce a simple line drawing of them.

3. Using a viewfinder, select an area of the line drawing to enlarge.

4. Divide the square sketch paper in to four equal sections using a pencil line.

5. Transfer the chosen area on to the four sections of square sketch paper, creating four identical images.

6. Add the same detail to each section by careful observation of the leaf patterns.

7. Add vibrant and contrasting colours to the design.

8. Cut along the pencil lines to produce the four separate identical designs.

9. Rotate the four identical designs and mount on paper.

55

Torn Paper Flowers

Resources
- A bunch of flowers
- Squares of magazine paper
- Glue
- A4 Sketch paper
- Sketch pencils
- Sequins
- Wool
- Fabric
- Craft straws
- Masking tape

Approach

1. Matisse's use of a variety of patterns and bold, vivid colours produces an exciting and inviting image.
2. Ask the children to choose a simple flower and from careful observation, do a line drawing.
3. Tear pieces of the magazine paper to use for collage work on the flower outline.
4. Select a piece of fabric for the centre of the flower.
5. Make sure to select bold, vivid colours to reflect Matisse's style.
6. Place the pieces of torn magazine paper on to the different sections of the flower outline.
7. Arrange the pieces so that they are overlapping to create texture.
8. Glue the pieces to the flower image.
9. Embellish the centre with sequins and pieces of wool.
10. Cut out the flower and tape to the straw.

Textile Still Life

Nature

Resources
- Calico (40cm^2)
- A selection of colourful fabrics, e.g. cotton, silk, velvet and linen
- Threads
- Needles
- Scissors
- Sequins, buttons and beads
- Printing materials, e.g. string, potato prints or polystyrene squares
- Paint or ink for printing
- Glue
- Tissue paper
- Foil

Approach

1. Look again at the painting *Seville Still Life*. Matisse's creative use of bright, contrasting colours and highly patterned designs produces a delightful and well-balanced composition.

2. Using the piece of calico, print a simple leaf design to create an effective background.

3. Choose a variety of suitable fabrics for the flowers, the vase and the tablecloth.

4. Make sure that the fabrics that are chosen reflect Matisse's style.

5. Cut out the tablecloth, flower and pot shapes.

6. Build up the composition by stitching the fabric on to the calico.

7. Embellish the surface with sequins, buttons and beads.

8. Add interest to the flowers by using tissue paper and foil.

57

Allina Khumalo Ndebele (1939–)

Mpisi and the Lion, 1992, (wool, hessian, thread) by Allina Khumalo Ndebele (1939–) Johannesburg Art Gallery, South Africa/Bridgeman Art Library © Johannesburg Art Gallery

Allina Khumalo Ndebele was born in KwaZulu-Natal in South Africa. She was taught spinning, weaving and design by two Swedish missionaries who went to South Africa to start a weaving workshop. Allina Ndebele's obvious artistic talent was recognised and in 1964 she received a scholarship to train in Sweden as a teacher weaver. She became a master weaver and in the late 1970s she returned to her father's village where she set up a workshop for weaving. The old Zulu myths and legends, told to her by her grandmother, have been a great source of inspiration and are depicted in her weavings. Her work is represented in public and private collections in Sweden, Germany and South Africa.

In her tapestry, *Mpisi and the Lion*, Allina Ndebele draws her inspiration from nature, which in turn inspires the earthy colours she has chosen for this piece of work. The lion is placed in a clearing in the middle of the tapestry and appears to be at the centre of his kingdom. His paws look like toes and his eyes are staring straight ahead. Surrounding the lion, different animals, people and birds have been woven into the background and foreground.

Coloured Paper Animal Designs

Nature

Resources
- A4 Coloured card in a variety of bright and lighter tones
- Three pieces of white card for templates (16cm width by 12cm length)
- Scissors
- Glue
- Sketch pencil
- Elephant, lion and zebra sketches
- Coloured card for mounting animal shapes (18½ cm width by 14½ cm length)

Approach

1. Look at Allina Ndebele's tapestry and ask the children to focus on the colours she uses. In this work, there are warm, bright colours alongside cooler blues and greys producing an interesting contrast.

2. Draw the outline of an elephant, zebra and lion on to the pieces of white card.

3. Cut out around the outlines to produce three templates.

4. Using the elephant template, draw its outline on three different coloured pieces of card. Cut out the elephant shapes.

5. Using a sketch pencil, draw two lines to divide each elephant into three sections. Make sure that the lines are drawn in the same place on each of the elephant shapes.

6. Cut along these lines to produce three sections per elephant.

7. Reassemble the elephants so that each one is made up of three different colours.

8. Glue the three parts on to a piece of mounting card, leaving a space between each one to create a pleasing design. Using the same process, create a design for the lion and the zebra shapes.

59

Animal Textile Wall Hanging

Resources
- Calico pieces (16½ cm width by 15½ cm length)
- Yellow, red and lilac wool
- Green, yellow and lilac sewing thread
- Needles
- Scissors
- Beads
- Embroidery thread
- Nine hessian pieces (20½ cm width by 19cm length)
- Large piece of calico
- Elephant, lion and zebra templates (from page 59)
- Glue
- Sketch pencils

Approach

1. Draw around the lion template (from page 59) with a sketch pencil on to three of the calico pieces.
2. Place the yellow wool over the pencil line of the lions and hold it in place.
3. Stitch over the wool using the contrasting green thread making small, straight stitches from one side to the other to hold the wool in place.
4. Using embroidery thread, fill in some details including the lions' manes, whiskers and faces.
5. Add detail to the lion's body using simple stitches with the embroidery thread.
6. As the embroidery thread is made up of six thin threads woven together, vary the thickness by separating them.
7. Use between one and six threads to create texture.
8. Glue or stitch beads in place for the eyes.
9. Using a simple sewing stitch, attach the three pieces of calico to the three pieces of hessian.
10. Use the same process for the elephants and the zebras.
11. Arrange the fabric pictures on to the larger piece of calico.
12. Using running stitches, attach the fabric pictures to the calico background.

Animal Cushions

Nature

Resources
- Scraps of brightly coloured fabrics
- Three calico pieces (17½ cm width by 16½ cm length)
- Three brightly coloured pieces of fabric 26cm^2
- Three calico backing pieces 26cm^2
- Fabric glue
- Sewing and embroidery threads
- Needle
- Three small buttons
- Scissors
- Soft pencil
- Animal templates
- Cushion pads 26cm^2

Approach

1. Place the zebra template on the reverse side of a strip of brightly coloured fabric.
2. Draw around the template with a soft pencil.
3. Cut out the zebra shape and glue or stitch it on to the piece of calico.
4. Glue or stitch the piece of calico on to the square of brightly coloured fabric to make the right side of the cushion cover.
5. Place the cushion cover, right sides together, with the calico-backing square.
6. Stitch the two pieces together, 1cm from the edge, leaving a 17cm opening at the bottom.
7. Turn the cushion cover the right side out.
8. Once the cushion is in place, fold the open edges together and stitch.
9. To embellish, glue or stitch on a small button for the zebra's eye.
10. Use the same process for the elephant and the lion.
11. In addition, for the lion, use embroidery thread to create a mane.
12. For the elephant, use embroidery thread to outline the ear.

Portraying Relationships

Paula Rego (1935–)

The Dance by Paula Rego (1935–) © Tate, London 2003

Paula Rego was born in Lisbon, Portugal. She studied at the Slade School of Art in London and while she was there she met her future husband, the artist Victor Willing, whom she married in 1959. She finds inspiration for her work from literature, fairy tales and nursery rhymes and is best known for her narrative paintings. The National Gallery, London, appointed her the first Associate Artist in 1990. She works from her studio in London and is recognised as one of the leading figurative artists at work today.

In this painting, *The Dance*, Paula Rego depicts the woman on the left as being larger-than-life. She demands our attention as she looks out of the painting whilst the other figures in the composition are engrossed in each other. The young couple near the centre are dancing close together and appear very happy, whereas the couple on the right, although they appear happy, are dancing slightly apart as the woman is obviously pregnant. The group behind them, comprising perhaps a child with her mother and grandmother, also seem to be enjoying themselves. The groups reflect the different stages in the woman's life.

Portraying Relationships

Pastel Dancers

From an early age, Paula Rego enjoyed drawing pictures about stories she had heard or taken from her imagination. In her painting, *The Dance*, we can clearly recognise the facial expressions of the figures. A variety of emotions are conveyed such as the obvious happiness of the young couples and the somewhat wistful expression of the solitary woman.

Resources
- A4 Black sugar paper
- A4 Black card
- Sketch pencil
- Oil pastels
- Silver pen
- Glue
- Scraps of fabric
- Scissors

Approach

1. Look at Paula Rego's painting and focus on the four groups of figures in the composition. Discuss what stage of life is represented in each group.
2. Choose one of the groups and sketch the figures on black sugar paper or card in the style of Paula Rego.
3. Draw in the folds of the woman's skirts to convey movement. Try to capture the expression in their faces.
4. Draw a silver moon in the night sky using a white oil pastel and outline it using a silver pen.
5. Using oil pastels, paint the background sky and landscape in dark blues and black to create the moonlit scene.
6. Using similar colours to Paula Rego, paint the sketch with the oil pastels.
7. Outline the figures in white pastel or silver pen to make them stand out.
8. Using a black oil pastel, emphasise the folds on the women's skirts to create an impression of movement.

The Mulberry Bush Dance

Paula Rego is fascinated and inspired by stories, storytelling and traditional nursery rhymes. She has produced many paintings depicting characters from nursery rhymes and children's stories such as Peter Pan, Pinocchio and Snow White. As a young child, she loved to dress up and to use her imagination.

Resources
- A4 Sketch paper
- Short pieces of string
- Poster paints
- Paintbrushes
- Video camera
- Glue
- Silver pen

Approach

1. Watch a group of younger children dancing the nursery rhyme, *The Mulberry Bush*. Alternatively, split the class in half and watch each other perform the rhyme.

2. Talk about how clothes swirl about and hair moves during the dance. Make a video of the children dancing and freeze-frame a selection of them to demonstrate this fact.

3. Experiment with paint on sketch paper, using different ways to apply it to convey movement, for example with fingers and with large, swirling brushstrokes.

4. Choose one of the freeze-frames from the video as a starting point and sketch the outline of three or more children dancing in a circle to the nursery rhyme, *The Mulberry Bush*.

5. Add colour to the sketch using poster paints.

6. Paint some short pieces of string using hair tones.

7. Glue the pieces of painted string on to the figures' heads in the painting, making sure they are arranged to show movement.

8. Outline the figures with a silver pen to create both a sense of unity and movement.

Portraying Relationships

The Dance

Paula Rego's painting, *The Dance*, was painted over a long period of time with many preliminary sketches done before the final painting was completed. The faces in her paintings clearly show a variety of emotions. Her style is very bold and expressive and she creates a sense of movement by emphasising the flowing folds in the women's skirts.

Approach

1. Look again at Paula Rego's composition, which depicts figures grouped individually, in twos and in threes.
2. Imagine that the setting is a modern-day dance or party with groups of children dancing on their own, in twos and in threes.
3. Using Paula Rego's style, draw an outline sketch on an acrylic painting board or white card, depicting a variety of groups dancing at a party.
4. Set the scene in a garden on a moonlit night.
5. Using acrylics, paint the background.
6. Paint the bodies of the dancing figures but not the heads.
7. Create a 3D effect for the dancers' heads by cutting up sections of tights.
8. Place some cotton wool inside the tights and wrap it in a circle, and tie a knot in the back to form the shape of a face.
9. Attach the face shapes to the painting with glue.
10. Paint the faces using acrylics.
11. Tear up pieces of magazine paper and glue on to the heads for the hair.

Resources
- A4 Acrylic painting board or white card
- Acrylic paints
- Paintbrushes
- Skin tone tights or stockings
- Cotton wool
- Sketch pencil
- Glue
- Scissors
- Magazine paper

David Hockney (1937–)

David Hockney "The Second Marriage" 1963, oil, gouache & collage on canvas 77 ¾×90" © David Hockney

David Hockney was born in the industrial town of Bradford in the north of England. He knew that he wanted to become an artist at a very early age and attended the Royal College of Art in 1959. He has produced a collection of double portraits. Portraiture particularly appeals to him because he is interested in the relationships between the people in them. He now lives in California in the United States of America. David Hockney is Britain's foremost living artist.

In his painting, *The Second Marriage*, David Hockney depicts a married couple who appear to be sitting in a somewhat box-like confined space. His picture has a three-dimensional quality through its irregular frame and contrasting sections of background, made from a mixture of paint and collage materials. The bridegroom is wearing a dark suit with sunglasses and looks rather severe. The bride is painted in profile and is wearing a white, fitted dress with pointed black shoes. They do not seem to be enjoying the occasion and the atmosphere is formal.

Portraying Relationships

Paper Collage Picture

Resources
- Magazine paper
- PVA glue
- Corrugated card
- Strips of black card
- Gold pen
- Black fine-line pen
- Scissors
- A4 card

Approach

1. Look at David Hockney's painting, *The Second Marriage,* and discuss the colours that he has used. How do these colours suggest the mood of the painting? Can the children describe the feelings of the couple, by looking at their expressions and the background environment?

2. Create a 3D model of Hockney's painting. First, build the background using larger pieces of paper and corrugated card to create a similar setting to Hockney's.

3. Cut out two pieces of card and arrange them to portray the box-like setting. Attach these to the A4 card with glue.

4. Cut out, from magazines, a section of paper that matches the colour of the sofa.

5. For the foreground, cut out strips of paper to match the carpet design.

6. Cut out a square for the table.

7. Arrange the pieces to match Hockney's composition and glue them in place.

8. For the figures, choose darker colours for the bridegroom and lighter ones for the bride.

9. Cut out and decorate the pieces from card and arrange to resemble the shapes of the two figures. Attach these to the scene.

10. Add extra detail using a gold pen and the fine-line pen.

Fabric and Paper Collage

Approach

1. Place the shoebox on its side and cut off the top section. Choose some patterned wrapping paper, cut it to fit the three sides of the box and glue it on.

2. Cut out pieces of fabric to match the rug and the carpet in Hockney's painting and stick them on.

3. Cut out a rectangular piece of cardboard to fit in the shoebox and bend it in half to make the shape of the sofa. Cut out a piece of fabric to fit over the cardboard base for the sofa and glue it on.

4. Using masking tape, cover some plastic bottle tops and stick them to the sofa to act as legs. Using the glue gun, stick the sofa to the floor.

5. For the tabletop, cut out a square of cardboard and attach four wooden craft sticks, using the glue gun. Stick the legs to the floor. For the curtains, roll up a strip of fabric, gather at the centre and tie with a thinner strip of the same material. Do the same for the other curtain.

6. Add detail to the room by sticking squares of fabric to the sofa as cushions. Cut a bottle shape out of black card, stick it on the table and add detail with a gold pen. To add further decoration, cut out a small rectangular piece of fabric, mount on a piece of black card and stick it to the wall with a piece of string.

7. For the bridegroom figure, cut a simple body shape out of black card and bend it in the middle. Add details to the figure using white card and the fine-line pen. Do the same for the bride using white card and glue on some string for the hair. Stick the figures to the sofa in a sitting position.

Resources
- Shoebox
- Glue gun
- PVA glue
- String
- Wooden craft sticks
- Gold pen
- Wrapping paper
- Cardboard
- Black and white card
- Plastic bottle tops
- Masking tape
- Scraps of fabric
- Black fine-line pen
- Scissors

Portraying Relationships

Group Portrait at a Wedding

Resources
- Wedding photographs
- A2 Thick white card
- Acrylic paints
- Paintbrushes (fine and thick)
- Masking tape
- Scraps of fabric
- Plasticine
- Gold and silver pens
- Sketch pencil
- Black fine-line pen
- White tissue paper
- Glue gun
- PVA glue
- Scissors
- Silver card

Approach

1. Talk about creating a contrasting picture to Hockney's. Use the theme of a modern wedding and brainstorm ideas with the children whilst looking at photographs of weddings.
2. Using the masking tape, attach the A2 card to a slightly larger surface such as a table or an easel.
3. Using the photograph as a starting point, draw a multiple figure sketch with the bride and bridegroom in the centre of the composition.
4. Sketch in the background including balloons, a champagne bottle and cork and some confetti.
5. Paint the background light blue and the foreground brown.
6. Using the plasticine, build up the objects in the background to give a 3D effect.
7. Cover the plasticine with tissue paper and glue and leave to dry.
8. Paint the figures in the picture, first adding detail with a silver pen. 
9. Using the fabrics, cut out the shapes of clothes and shoes and glue on.
10. Paint the figures' skin using the acrylics.
11. For the bride's dress, paint it white and then apply strips of tissue paper with glue to create a 3D effect.
12. Paint the balloons, confetti, champagne bottle and cork and add detail with the gold and silver pens.
13. Add the final details to the faces using the fine-line pen.
14. A collaborative approach would be ideal for this painting with perhaps three or four children working together.
15. Remove the masking tape and add a frame to the finished picture made from silver card.

Gary Blythe (1959–)

Illustration from *THE WHALES' SONG* by Dyan Sheldon published by Red Fox. Used by permission of The Random House Group Limited.

Gary Blythe was born in Liverpool and studied illustration at the Liverpool Polytechnic, England. He has made a very successful career illustrating picture books. His best-selling book, *The Whales' Song*, won the highly prestigious Kate Greenaway Award for illustration in the UK. He has worked on many other well-known children's picture books and in his spare time, enjoys painting, drawing and observing. He lives in Merseyside with his wife.

In this illustration from *The Whales' Song*, Gary Blythe depicts the close relationship between Lilly and her grandmother. Lilly is listening intently to her grandmother's story about how, as a child, she used to sit on the jetty and listen out for the whales. Lilly is enthralled by the story and her expression of wonder has been portrayed perfectly through Gary Blythe's use of facial expression. The contrast between the two faces is a dramatic one. The grandmother's kindly lined face is framed by her wispy grey hair, whereas Lilly's face, with her large trusting eyes and dark, curly hair, presents a very touching image.

Portraying Relationships

Double Portraits in Watercolour and String

Resources
- A4 and A5 Sketch paper
- Watercolour paints
- Paintbrushes (fine and thick)
- Sketch pencils
- Digital camera
- Photographs showing two people
- PVA glue
- Scissors
- String
- Poster paint (yellow, black and brown)

Approach

1. Look at a range of photographs, which show two people interacting. Discuss how their clothes, expressions, gestures and relative size are used to convey ideas about their relationships.

2. Read *The Whales' Song* and focus particularly on Gary Blythe's illustration of Lilly and her grandmother. Talk about how their expressions convey how happy they are in each other's company.

3. Ask the children to pose for a photograph in twos. Make sure that there is a clear link between them, such as sharing a book or playing a game of cards. Take a photograph of the pose.

4. Using the photograph as a starting point, ask the children to sketch the image.

5. Develop the sketch into a larger picture of the two figures. Using watercolours, paint the composition.

6. Cut some string into short pieces. Paint the pieces of string using yellow, black and brown paint and allow to dry.

7. Stick the string on to the figures as hair to add a 3D element to the work.

A Portrait of Lilly and her Grandmother

Approach

1. Re-read the story, *The Whales' Song*. Afterwards, look at Gary Blythe's illustration of Lilly and her grandmother and discuss the story that the characters are sharing.

2. Ask the children to produce a basic sketch of Lilly and her grandmother.

3. Using chalk pastels, add colour to the sketch but do not paint the hair at this stage. Pick out the finer details with a black chalk pastel. Spray with fixative.

4. For the grandmother's hair, mix white and black poster paint to make grey. Add sand to the paint to create more texture and paint on thickly.

5. For Lilly's hair, add PVA glue to black and brown paint. Apply the paint using swirling brush strokes.

6. Finally, add some white paint to highlight the lighter tones in Lilly's hair.

Resources
- PVA glue
- Sand
- Poster paint (black, white and brown)
- Paintbrushes (thick and fine)
- Fixative
- Sketch pencils
- Chalk pastels
- A4 White card